COVER STORY

Hollywood Fan Magazines of the 1940s

Pomegranate

SAN FRANCISCO

Pomegranate Communications, Inc.
Box 6099
Rohnert Park, CA 94927
www.pomegranate.com

Pomegranate Europe Ltd.
Fullbridge House, Fullbridge
Maldon, Essex CM9 4LE
England

ISBN 0-7649-0942-8
Pomegranate Catalog No. A958

Pomegranate publishes books of
postcards on a wide range of subjects.
Please write for more information.

Designed by Shannon Lemme
Printed in China
09 08 07 06 05 04 03 02 01 00   10 9 8 7 6 5 4 3 2

To facilitate detachment of the postcards from this book, fold each card along its perforation line before tearing.

From the earliest days of motion pictures, the American public has had an insatiable interest in film stars. The first fan magazine, *Photoplay*, appeared in 1911, presenting movie scenarios and predating the first feature-length film. By the 1930s, fan magazines focused on performers' looks, personalities, families, and private lives. They were liberally illustrated with star portraits and "candid" shots that look every bit as posed as the portraits. The prose style fell somewhere between winking flattery and outrageous hyperbole. Contributing writers included Hollywood gossip columnists Hedda Hopper and Louella Parsons, and—with ghostwritten texts—the featured stars.

The magazines were aimed at the female matinee audience, as the advertisements for lingerie, deodorant creams, and hair ointments attest. While divorces were duly reported, the policy was to soften scandal, with actors encouraged to counter even the mildest allegations. The stars were made to seem approachable, full of sage advice and homely virtues. Male stars showed a modest pleasure in their hobbies—amateur chemistry and the accordion for James Stewart—while female stars trumpeted the glories of married life and motherhood.

Photoplay lasted until 1980, but most of the classic Hollywood fan magazines were gone by the 1970s; their spirit lives on in publications like *People, In Style,* and *Vanity Fair,* which regularly feature cover stories on actors and other entertainment-industry figures.

The magazines featured in this volume are part of the 80,000-item collection of film and television artifacts—one of the largest of its kind in the world—housed by the American Museum of the Moving Image. Some of the materials in the collection, such as costumes, props, and special-effects makeup, can be seen on the screen. Many more illustrate the world of work behind the screen: cameras and other technical apparatus, set designs, behind-the-scenes photographs. Others reveal the ways in which the film and television industries connect with their audience: posters, pressbooks, licensed merchandise, and, of course, fan magazines.

The magazines illustrated in this book were all donated by one collector, Naomi Beckley, whose gift of 1,500 fan magazines included every copy of every popular title from 1939 through 1950.

—Rochelle Slovin, Director of the American Museum of the Moving Image

PHOTOPLAY

combined with Movie Mirror

November

15¢

Judy Garland
By Paul Hesse

COVER STORY

Judy Garland (1922–1969)
Photoplay, November 1945

This issue of *Photoplay* commemorated the election of Judy Garland by the French Congress of Fashions as "the smartest woman in the world in the matter of clothes in the year 1945." Garland, recently married to Vincente Minnelli, was starring in *The Harvey Girls*.

Pomegranate

BOX 6099   ROHNERT PARK   CA 94927

MOVIE STORY

MAGAZINE

OCTOBER
15¢

COVER STORY

Katharine Hepburn (b. 1907) and **Robert Taylor** (1911–1969)
Movie Story Magazine, October 1946

Vincente Minnelli's thriller *Undercurrent* was one of the low
points of Hepburn's career during the forties, a decade in
which she was successfully paired with Spencer Tracy. The film
did further the career of rising star Robert Mitchum, who had
a supporting role.

Pomegranate

BOX 6099   ROHNERT PARK   CA 94927

MOTION PICTURE

A FAWCETT PUBLICATION

MAGAZINE

OCTOBER
15¢

LENA HORNE

LEW AYRES' SIDE OF THE STORY -- BY CABLE FROM NEW GUINEA
INTIMATE CLOSE-UP OF LENA HORNE BY SIDNEY SKOLSKY

COVER STORY

Lena Horne (b. 1917)
Motion Picture Magazine, October 1944

Singer, actress, and "a favorite pin-up girl with all members
of the Armed Forces," Horne was written up as the only
African American actress who "sustained a career in
Hollywood movies without becoming a comedy character
or portraying servants."

Pomegranate

BOX 6099   ROHNERT PARK   CA 94927

PDC

Movie Life

DECEMBER

10¢

IN USA and CANADA

ABBOTT-COSTELLO'S MILLION DOLLAR SECRET!
RITA HAYWORTH'S LIFE STORY TOLD IN PICTURES

COVER STORY

Lou Costello (1906–1959) and **Bud Abbott** (1895–1974)
Movie Life, December 1941

Straight man Bud Abbott and his frantic sidekick, Lou Costello, were a highly successful comedy team in the forties and early fifties, making four films in 1941 alone. This issue of *Movie Life* reported on their supply of 28,000 gags from their days in burlesque.

Pomegranate BOX 6099 ROHNERT PARK CA 94927

SCREENLAND

MAY

15¢

BACALL'S Slant on BOGART!

Joan Fontaine

COVER STORY

Joan Fontaine (b. 1917)
Screenland, May 1945

Known for her tremulous performances in Hitchcock's *Rebecca* (1940) and *Suspicion* (1941), and for her troubled relationship with sister Olivia de Havilland, Fontaine was starring in *The Affairs of Susan* at the time this cover appeared.

Pomegranate

BOX 6099   ROHNERT PARK   CA 94927

FLAMINGO ROAD starring JOAN CRAWFORD and ZACHARY SCOTT

MOVIE STORY

JUNE • 15 CENTS

THE GREAT
SINNER

starring
GREGORY PECK
AVA GARDNER

COVER STORY

Ava Gardner (1922–1990) and **Gregory Peck** (b. 1916)
Movie Story, June 1949

Celebrated for his heroic roles in literary adaptations, Peck played no less than Dostoyevsky himself in *The Great Sinner* opposite Gardner, then between marriages to Artie Shaw and Frank Sinatra.

Pomegranate

BOX 6099   ROHNERT PARK   CA 94927

Movie Life

PDC

MARCH
15c

LUCILLE
BALL

MOVIE LIFE OF LUCILLE BALL
SONNY TUFTS' AMAZING STORY

COVER STORY

Lucille Ball (1911–1989)
Movie Life, March 1944

Before she became America's best-loved television comedian, Lucille Ball starred in a variety of movie dramas, musicals, and comedies. *Movie Life* told her life story in pictures, including baby portraits, a photo-filmography, and snapshots of her 1940 wedding to Desi Arnaz.

Pomegranate

BOX 6099   ROHNERT PARK   CA 94927

Modern Screen

OCTOBER
15¢

A DELL MAGAZINE
DELL
A DELL MAGAZINE

FRANK SINATRA

COVER STORY

Frank Sinatra (1915–1998)
Modern Screen, October 1945

Modern Screen's feature on the making of Sinatra's
Academy Award-winning anti-bigotry short, *The House I
Live In*, portrayed the singing heartthrob as a real-life
paragon of liberal virtue, prone to preaching tolerance to
Brooklyn street punks over spaghetti dinners.

Pomegranate

BOX 6099   ROHNERT PARK   CA 94927

PHOTOPLAY

October

15¢

Lana Turner
By Paul Hesse

COVER STORY

Lana Turner (1920–1995)
Photoplay, October 1946

The subject of one of Hollywood's greatest "discovery" legends, Turner was shown in *Photoplay* cavorting with her three-year-old daughter Cheryl Crane. Twelve years later, Crane precipitated a front-page scandal by stabbing her mother's gangster lover, Johnny Stompanato, to death.

Pomegranate   BOX 6099   ROHNERT PARK   CA 94927

MOVIE STORY

MAGAZINE

SEPTEMBER
15c

Exclusive!

NOTORIOUS

Starring

CARY GRANT and INGRID BERGMAN

COVER STORY

Ingrid Bergman (1915–1982) and **Cary Grant** (1904–1986)
Movie Story Magazine, September 1946

One of Alfred Hitchcock's most sophisticated and accomplished films, Notorious starred Bergman as a good-time girl who marries a spy in order to help the American agent she loves (Grant). The two engage in a kiss of record length, stopping and starting several times in order to foil the censors.

Pomegranate   BOX 6099   ROHNERT PARK   CA 94927

MODERN SCREEN

MAY
10
CENTS

BARBARA STANWYCK

HUNDREDS OF INTIMATE PHOTOS OF YOUR SCREEN FAVORITES!

COVER STORY

Barbara Stanwyck (1907–1990)
Modern Screen, May 1941

Barbara Stanwyck, often considered the consummate professional, starred in two of her most memorable films—Frank Capra's *Meet John Doe* and Preston Sturges's *The Lady Eve*—in 1941. Three years later, the Internal Revenue Service announced that she was the highest-paid woman in the United States, just ahead of Bette Davis.

Pomegranate   BOX 6099   ROHNERT PARK   CA 94927

Motion Picture

MAGAZINE ©

JANUARY
15ᶜ

JAMES STEWART
BY MEAD-MADDICK

COVER STORY

James Stewart (1908–1997)
Motion Picture Magazine, January 1947

Stewart returned from World War II "still in the market for a wife," as *Motion Picture* described him on the eve of the release of *It's a Wonderful Life*. Two years later, he wed Gloria Hatrick McLean; their marriage lasted forty-five years.

Pomegranate

BOX 6099   ROHNERT PARK   CA 94927

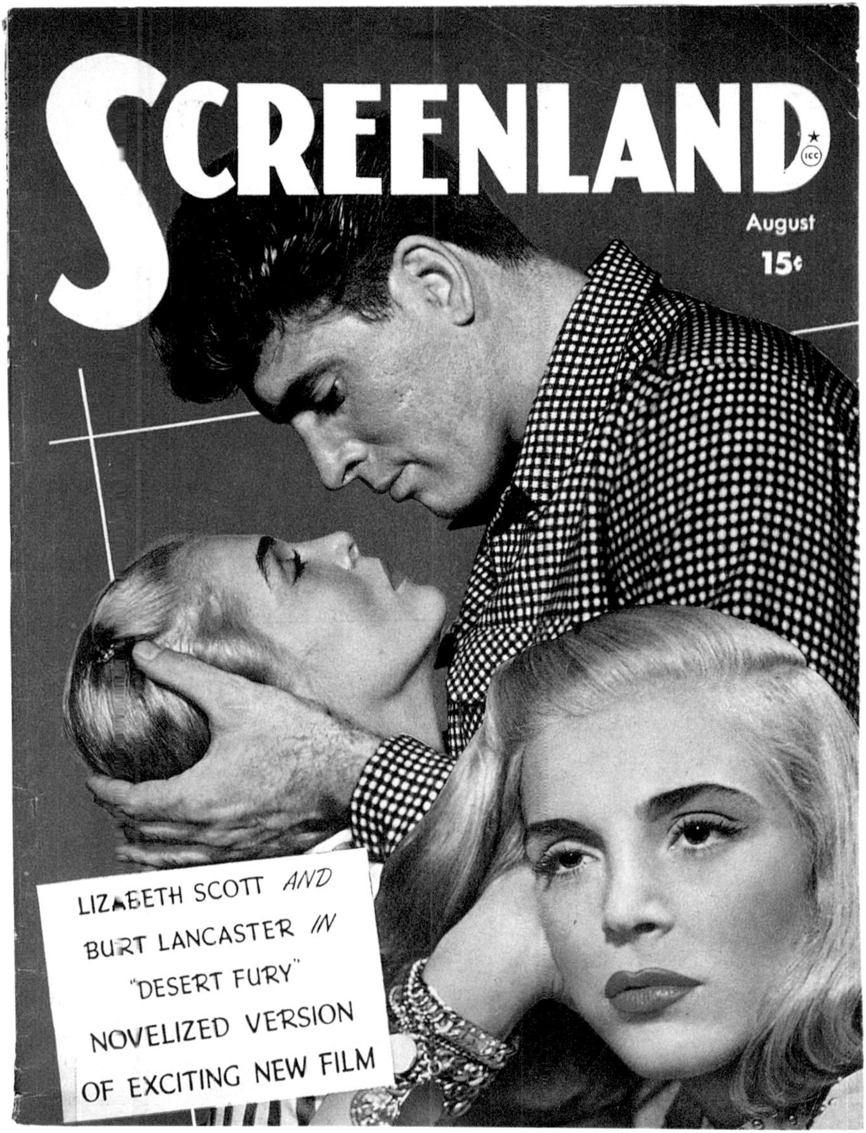
SCREENLAND
ICC
August
15¢
LIZABETH SCOTT AND
BURT LANCASTER IN
"DESERT FURY"
NOVELIZED VERSION
OF EXCITING NEW FILM

COVER STORY

Lizabeth Scott (b. 1922) and **Burt Lancaster** (1913–1994)
Screenland, August 1947

Screenland drummed up interest in the upcoming *Desert Fury* with a "fictionized" photo story of the movie, followed by an account of the recent marriage of Lancaster, who had achieved stardom the year before in *The Killers*.

Pomegranate   BOX 6099   ROHNERT PARK   CA 94927

PHOTOPLAY

combined with Movie Mirror

March

15¢

Gene Tierney
By Paul Hesse

Eleven Beautiful Full-Color Pages of Star Portraits and Fashions

COVER STORY

Gene Tierney (1920–1991)
Photoplay, March 1946

Gene Tierney stepped out of the icily serene persona
she had established in films such as *Laura* (1944) to play
the murderously selfish heroine of *Leave Her to Heaven,*
based on a best-selling novel.

Pomegranate

BOX 6099 ROHNERT PARK CA 94927

ONLY 5 CENT MOVIE MAGAZINE IN THE WORLD

Hollywood

SCREEN LIFE

A FAWCETT PUBLICATION

HOLLYWOOD
5¢

FEBRUARY

CLARK GABLE
VIVIEN LEIGH in
"GONE WITH THE WIND"

IS VIVIEN LEIGH A REAL-LIFE SCARLETT O'HARA?

COVER STORY

Vivien Leigh (1913–1967) and **Clark Gable** (1901–1960)
Hollywood/Screen Life, February 1940

According to the story in this issue, Leigh's resemblance to her most famous role was more than skin deep: like Scarlett O'Hara, Leigh went "from pampered young beauty . . . through a marriage contracted more from pride than passion, to a well-earned triumph over personal and professional problems."

Pomegranate

BOX 6099   ROHNERT PARK   CA 94927

OCTOBER · 25¢

Screen
Guide

A HILLMAN PUBLICATION

Rita Hayworth

EXPOSED! DRAMATIC AND MODELING SCHOOL RACKETS

COVER STORY

Rita Hayworth (1918–1987)
Screen Guide, October 1947

Hayworth is shown here in a cosmetic aberration: the short blonde hair Orson Welles had convinced her to wear in the forthcoming *The Lady from Shanghai*. By the time this magazine came out, Welles and Hayworth were already divorced, and Hayworth had returned to her characteristic shoulder-length red locks.

Pomegranate

BOX 6099   ROHNERT PARK   CA 94927

SCREENLAND

ANC

September

15¢

Gary Cooper and
Patricia Neal

Ann
Sothern
tells

How To
Attract
YOUR
Prince
Charming

COVER STORY

Patricia Neal (b. 1926) and **Gary Cooper** (1901–1961)
Screenland, September 1949

This cover of a passionate embrace between Cooper and Neal, co-starring in King Vidor's film of Ayn Rand's novel *The Fountainhead*, was deceptive; *Screenland* made no mention in its pages of the film, its stars, or their otherwise well-publicized love affair.

Pomegranate

BOX 6099   ROHNERT PARK   CA 94927

Screen
Guide

A HILLMAN PUBLICATION

SEPTEMBER
25 CENTS

Scoops!

FIRST COLOR ON VIC DAMONE

ESTHER WILLIAMS IN HAWAII

Photo Stories: **BETTY GRABLE**

LANA TURNER, KIRK DOUGLAS

ESTHER WILLIAMS

COVER STORY

Esther Williams (b. 1923)
Screen Guide, September 1950

Swimming star Williams, Hollywood's "million dollar mermaid," was captured for *Screen Guide* on location in Hawaii for *Pagan Love Story*.

Pomegranate   BOX 6099   ROHNERT PARK   CA 94927

MODERN SCREEN

SEPTEMBER

10

CENTS

THE LARGEST
CIRCULATION
OF ANY SCREEN
MAGAZINE

ASTA
and
MYRNA LOY

WHAT'S THE MATTER WITH LOMBARD?

COVER STORY

Myrna Loy (1905–1993)
Modern Screen, September 1939

Myrna Loy provided the perfect foil to William Powell in the six *Thin Man* movies. Their urbane crime-solving team would not have been complete without the wire-haired terrier Asta, a star in his own right.

Pomegranate

BOX 6099   ROHNERT PARK   CA 94927

MOVIES

FEBRUARY

25c

CORNEL
WILDE

SINATRA
& FAMILY
*Intimate Home
Photos*

COVER STORY

Cornel Wilde (1915–1989)
Movies, February 1948

Florid matinee idol Cornel Wilde was best known for his swashbuckling and period roles, particularly in *A Song to Remember* (1945) and *Forever Amber* (1947).

Pomegranate

BOX 6099   ROHNERT PARK   CA 94927

P.D.C.

MOVIE STARS
PARADE

Gene Autry vs. *Roy Rogers* -THE TRUTH!

HOW HOLLYWOOD GIRLS STACK UP - *Jeff Lynn*

March **10¢**

in U.S.A. and Canada

VERONICA LAKE

COVER STORY

Veronica Lake (1919–1973)
Movie Stars Parade, March 1942

Peekaboo Girl Veronica Lake, appearing in Preston
Sturges's great Hollywood sendup *Sullivan's Travels*, was
soon to make her contribution to the war effort by cutting
off her trademark fall of hair, which had become a hazard to
the female factory workers who copied it.

Pomegranate   BOX 6099   ROHNERT PARK   CA 94927

Motion Picture

MAGAZINE ©

May

Only
10c

JANE RUSSELL

*What Broke Up
Dick Haymes'
Marriage?*

COVER STORY

Errol Flynn (1909–1959)
Modern Screen, November 1943

The most popular swashbuckling star of the thirties and forties, Flynn matched his on-screen adventures with his off-screen exploits. However, *Modern Screen* "exposed" only "a homey guy with an insatiable yen for his big white farmhouse and a sweet-toothed nag named Onyx."

Pomegranate

BOX 6099   ROHNERT PARK   CA 94927

THEY GIVE LIVES—YOU LEND MONEY!

MODERN SCREEN

NOVEMBER
15¢

DELL

ERROL FLYNN

Errol Flynn
EXPOSED!

COVER STORY

Errol Flynn (1909–1959)
Modern Screen, November 1943

The most popular swashbuckling star of the thirties and forties, Flynn matched his on-screen adventures with his off-screen exploits. However, *Modern Screen* "exposed" only "a homey guy with an insatiable yen for his big white farmhouse and a sweet-toothed nag named Onyx."

Pomegranate   BOX 6099   ROHNERT PARK   CA 94927

PHOTOPLAY

combined with Movie Mirror

June

15¢

Lauren Bacall
By Paul Hesse

SEVENTH
WAR LOAN DRIVE
See 5-Star letter
on page 27

COVER STORY

Lauren Bacall (b. 1924)
Photoplay, June 1945

At the time of her *Photoplay* cover, Bacall was starring in
The Big Sleep, her greatest collaboration with Humphrey
Bogart, coyly referred to here as "her favorite guy." They
married just as this issue hit the stands.

Pomegranate

BOX 6099   ROHNERT PARK   CA 94927

PHOTOPLAY

combined with Movie Mirror

October

15¢

Maureen O'Hara
By Paul Hesse

COVER STORY

Maureen O'Hara (b. 1920)
Photoplay, October 1945

Maureen O'Hara made her mark as the high-spirited heroine of adventure movies such as *The Spanish Main*, her upcoming film at the time of this interview, which described her home life while husband Will Price was at war.

Pomegranate

BOX 6099   ROHNERT PARK   CA 94927

MOVIE STORY

MAGAZINE

A Fawcett Publication

MARCH
15c

LANA TURNER
JOHN GARFIELD
IN

"THE POSTMAN
ALWAYS RINGS TWICE"

COVER STORY

Lana Turner (1920–1995) and **John Garfield** (1913–1952)
Movie Story Magazine, March 1946

Tay Garnett's steamy adaptation of James M. Cain's crime novel *The Postman Always Rings Twice* brought Turner and Garfield together for a memorable clinch on the beach, a prelude to murder.

Pomegranate   BOX 6099   ROHNERT PARK   CA 94927

MOVIE STARS

PARADE

DECEMBER
15¢

DEANNA DURBIN

PLEDGE YOURSELF TO BUY
U. S. WAR BONDS REGULARLY

Jeanette MacDonald's **TIPS TO GIRLS ON THE HOME FRONT**

COVER STORY

Deanna Durbin (b. 1921)
Movie Stars Parade, December 1942

A classically trained singing prodigy, Durbin began her movie career at the age of fourteen in 1936. This cover story marked Durbin's return to the screen after a year-long suspension following a battle with the studio for greater control over her movies. Her upcoming first "grown-up" picture, *Forever Yours*, featured serious subject matter and a more polished look for Durbin.

Pomegranate

BOX 6099   ROHNERT PARK   CA 94927

MOVIE
STARS
PARADE

SEPTEMBER
15¢

FDC

HEDY LAMARR

$1,000 PRIZE CONTEST

My Favorite Gags BY BOB HOPE

COVER STORY

Hedy Lamarr (b. 1913)
Movie Stars Parade, September 1943

Known for her nude appearance in the Czech film *Ecstasy* (1933), Hedy Lamarr was one of Hollywood's most glamorous imports from Europe. In 1940, Lamarr, who had learned about weaponry from her first husband, a munitions magnate, worked with composer George Antheil to create an anti-jamming device for the Allies that served as the foundation for today's secure military communications.

Modern Screen

APRIL
15¢

DELL
A DELL MAGAZINE

SUSAN HAYWA
BARRY SULLIVA
BEULAH BONDI CECIL KELLA

A Paramount Picture

ADD
LAKE

LA

COVER STORY

Alan Ladd (1913–1964)
Modern Screen, April 1946

Starring in his third *film noir* with Veronica Lake, *The Blue Dahlia*, Ladd played a hard-boiled hero who could not have been more different from the Ladd described by *Modern Screen*, in loving detail, as a model boss to his two devoted secretaries.

Pomegranate   BOX 6099   ROHNERT PARK   CA 94927

MOVIE STARS
PARADE

An IDEAL Magazine

SEPTEMBER

15¢

PDC

SUSAN
HAYWARD

COVER STORY

Susan Hayward (1918–1975)
Movie Stars Parade, September 1944

This cover was important publicity for Hayward, who was about to make the transition from playing second-lead roles to starring in the tearjerkers for which she is best remembered.

Pomegranate

BOX 6099   ROHNERT PARK   CA 94927